12/09

W9-AZB-778

Sprouting Seed Science Projects

ANN BENBOW AND COLIN MABLY

ILLUSTRATIONS BY TOM LABAFF

Enslow Elementary

an imprint of

Enslow Publishers, Inc.

40 Industrial Road
Box 398
Berkeley Heights, NJ 07922
USA

http://www.enslow.com

Enslow Elementary, an imprint of Enslow Publishers, Inc.

Enslow Elementary® is a registered trademark of Enslow Publishers, Inc.

Library of Congress Cataloging-in-Publication Data

Benbow, Ann.
   Sprouting seed science projects / Ann Benbow and Colin Mably.
     p. cm. — (Real life science experiments)
   Includes bibliographical references and index.
   Summary: "Presents several easy-to-do science experiments using plants"—Provided by publisher.
   ISBN-13: 978-0-7660-3147-0
   ISBN-10: 0-7660-3147-0
   1. Seeds—Experiments—Juvenile literature. 2. Germination—Experiments—Juvenile literature.
   3. Seed—projects—Juvenile literature. I. Mably, Colin. II. Title.
   QK661.B38 2009
   580.78—dc22
                        2008001731

Printed in the United States of America

10 9 8 7 6 5 4 3 2 1

To Our Readers: We have done our best to make sure all Internet Addresses in this book were active and appropriate when we went to press. However, the authors and the publisher have no control over and assume no liability for the material available on those Internet sites or on other Web sites they may link to. Any comments or suggestions can be sent by e-mail to comments@enslow.com or to the address on the back cover.

♻ Enslow Publishers, Inc., is committed to printing our books on recycled paper. The paper in every book contains 10% to 30% post-consumer waste (PCW). The cover board on the outside of each book contains 100% PCW. Our goal is to do our part to help young people and the environment too!

Illustration Credits: Tom LaBaff

Photo Credits: © Alabama Department of Archives and History, Montgomery, p. 28; NASA Marshall Space Flight Center, p. 24; © Nigel Cattlin/Visuals Unlimited, p. 20; Shutterstock, pp. 8, 12, 16, 32, 36, 40, 44.

Cover Photo: F. Stuart Westmorland/Photo Researchers, Inc.

Contents

Experiments with a 🎗 symbol feature **Ideas for Your Science Fair.**

Introduction

Many kinds of plants make seeds. Each seed has a baby plant inside it. The seed also has food for the baby plant and a tough coat to protect it. Some kinds of plants that make seeds are radishes, oak trees, and sunflowers. Many plants grow their seeds inside fruits.

People and other animals use many kinds of seeds for food. You might like to eat peanuts, popcorn, or pumpkin seeds. Seeds from wheat plants are ground into flour for bread. Sesame seeds add crunch to hamburger buns. You might see squirrels eating acorns, or birds eating seeds from a feeder.

You can use this book to investigate many things about seeds. You will be asking questions about seeds and doing experiments with them. You will make observations and find answers. By the end, you will know a lot about seeds.

Science Fair Ideas

The investigations in this book will help you learn how to do experiments. After every investigation, you will find ideas for science fair projects. You may want to try one of these ideas, or you might think of a better project.

This book has a Learn More section. The books and Web sites in this section can give you more ideas for science fair projects.

Remember, science is all about asking questions. A science fair gives you the chance to investigate your own questions and record your results. It also lets you share your findings with your fellow scientists.

Safety First!

These are important rules to follow as you experiment.

1 Always have an adult nearby when doing experiments.

2 Follow instructions with care, especially safety warnings.

3 Never experiment with electrical outlets.

4 Use safety scissors, and have an adult handle any sharp objects.

5 Use only alcohol thermometers, never mercury!

6 Stay in a safe place if making outdoor observations.

7 Treat living things with care. Some may sting or be poisonous!

8 Keep your work area clean and organized.

9 Clean up and put materials away when you are done.

10 Always wash your hands when you are finished.

Experiment 1
What Is in a Seed?

What do you think is inside a seed? Write down your ideas and your reasons for them.

Now Let's Find Out!

1 Put 3 lima bean seeds and 3 corn seeds into a cup of water. Let them soak overnight.

Things You Will Need

an adult
3 lima bean seeds
3 corn seeds
cup of water
paper towels
3 zip-closing plastic bags
knife
magnifier
pencil and paper

2 Put a piece of paper towel into each of 3 zip-closing plastic bags. Put the 3 lima bean seeds in one bag and the 3 corn seeds in the other. Zip the bags almost shut and put them in a dark place until they sprout. (Keep the paper towel damp, and leave the plastic bag a little open so that the seeds do not get moldy.) Check them every day.

3 When they sprout, **ask an adult** to cut the seeds in half
   lengthwise.

4 Use your magnifier to look at the cut parts of the seeds.
   Draw what you see inside.

5 How are the lima bean and the corn seeds the same?
   How are they different? Do you have any ideas about
   what the seed parts do?

What Is in a Seed?

An Explanation

Each plant seed contains a baby plant (embryo) and food for that embryo to grow. In corn, the food is the endosperm. In beans, the food is stored in the seed leaves (cotyledons). There is also a seed coat to protect what is inside the seed. You might have noticed that there were two seed leaves in the lima bean, and only one very small one in the corn seed.

Plants with one seed leaf are called monocots. Plants with two seed leaves are called dicots. These are the two

FACT: One third of all the world's flowering plants are monocots. The largest family of monocots in the world is the orchid family.

main groups of plants. Other examples of monocots are grasses, lilies, and onions. Examples of dicots are maples, oaks, geraniums, dandelions, and roses.

 ## Ideas for Your Science Fair

- How are monocot seeds different from dicot seeds? How are they the same?

- How are monocot leaves different from dicot leaves? How are they the same?

- What other differences can you observe between monocots and dicots?

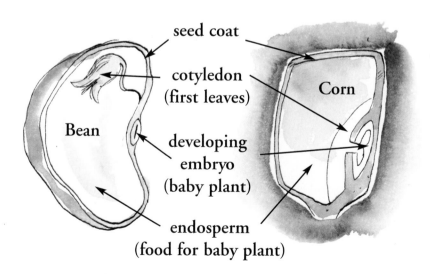

seed coat

cotyledon
(first leaves)

Corn

Bean

developing
embryo
(baby plant)

endosperm
(food for baby plant)

Experiment 2
How Are Seeds the Same and Different?

Do all seeds have the same types of parts? Write down your ideas and your reasons for them.

Now Let's Find Out!

1 Look carefully at a variety of seeds with your magnifying glass. What parts do all the seeds seem to have? (Look very carefully at the corn seed, since you will be popping a corn seed later.)

2 Look again at all the seeds. **Ask an adult** to cut some of them open very carefully. (Some seeds may be too tough to cut.) How are the cut seeds the same or different from one another?

Things You Will Need

an adult

variety of seeds (popcorn, grass, acorns, maple, bean, marigold, pumpkin, avocado)

knife (to open seeds)

magnifying glass

microwave oven

packet of microwave popcorn

pencil and paper

10

3 Following the instructions on the package, cook a bag of popcorn in the microwave. Look at the kernels of popped corn carefully. What is the white puffy part of each kernel?

4 What other seed parts can you find on a piece of popcorn?

How Are Seeds the Same and Different?

An Explanation

Seeds from flowering plants have the same basic parts. They can, however, be different in many ways. Some, like the avocado seed and the acorn, have tough coats. Seeds can be tiny or large. Burrs, coconuts, and maple seeds look like seeds, but they are fruits with seeds inside them.

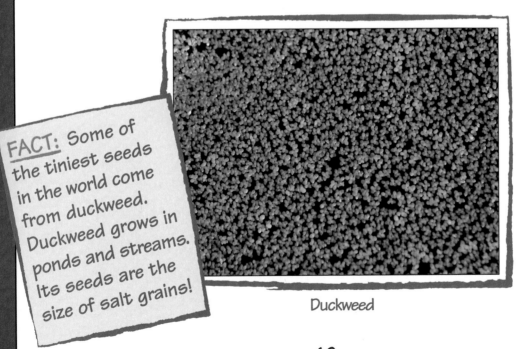

FACT: Some of the tiniest seeds in the world come from duckweed. Duckweed grows in ponds and streams. Its seeds are the size of salt grains!

Duckweed

12

Popcorn is able to pop because the microwave oven heats up the water inside the corn seed until the seed explodes. The white puffy part of the popcorn is the food stored inside the seed.

Ideas for Your Science Fair

- Will smaller seeds sprout sooner than larger seeds?
- Do different brands of popcorn expand to the same amount?
- Will marigold seeds sprout more quickly if they are soaked overnight first?

Red beans   Burrs   Coconut   Maple seeds

13

Experiment 3
How Do Seeds Get Around?

To grow, many kinds of seeds have to sprout far from their parent plants. How do you think these seeds travel? Write down your ideas and your reasons for them.

Now Let's Find Out!

Things You Will Need

different seeds (for example, maple, grass, dandelion, lima bean, acorn, coconut, apple, sweet gum, burr)

magnifying glass

pencil and paper

small battery-powered fan

bowl of water

poster paper and markers

1 Line up all the seeds you have gathered. Look at them with a magnifying glass. Do these seeds have any parts that look like they might help seeds travel? Write down, or draw a picture of, your ideas.

2 Can some seeds get blown by the wind? Use a fan to test your idea.

14

3   Could some of your seeds travel by falling into rivers and get carried away? Which seeds seem likely to float on water? Use a bowl of water to test your idea. Which seeds float? Which sink?

4   Which of your seeds might travel by being eaten or stuck on an animal's fur? Why do you think that? What are other ways you think seeds might travel?

5   When you finish, make a poster showing your seeds and your discoveries of how they could travel from place to place.

How Do Seeds Get Around?

An Explanation

Seeds can travel in many different ways. Some seeds, such as maple seeds and dandelion seeds, are very light. They have special parts that help them float on the wind. Other seeds, especially those in tasty fruits, get eaten by animals and left behind with the animals' waste. Still other seeds can fall into water and float to new places. Seeds with sticky parts on them, such as sweet gum and burrs, can end

FACT: The mistletoe plant attaches itself to trees. Birds can carry mistletoe seeds to new trees. They eat the seeds and then leave them in their droppings. The dropped seeds then begin to grow into new plants.

Mistletoe growing on a tree

up on the fur of animals, and then get dropped far away. Milkweed pods and cattail spikes "explode" to release the seeds and give them a boost into the air.

 ## Ideas for Your Science Fair

- How do the seeds from plants in your yard (or the school's yard) get around?

- Which seeds are most easily blown by the wind?

- Which seeds are likely to be eaten by birds or rodents, and why?

Seeds carried by wind

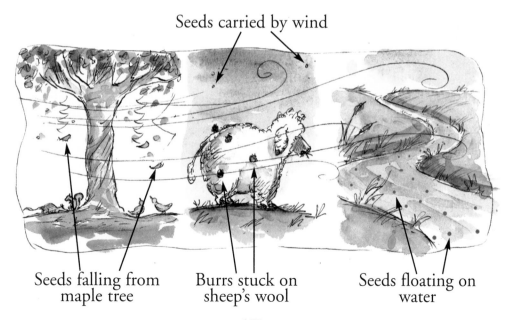

Seeds falling from maple tree

Burrs stuck on sheep's wool

Seeds floating on water

How Long Do Different Seeds Take to Sprout?

Do you think that all seeds sprout in the same amount of time? Write down your ideas and your reasons for them.

Now Let's Find Out!

1 Look at lima bean, radish, grass, and cucumber seeds with a magnifying glass. Which seed might be quickest to start growing? Which might be slowest? Write down the reasons for your answers.

Things You Will Need

packets of lima bean, radish, grass, and cucumber seeds

magnifying glass

marker, pencil, and paper

4 foam cups

potting soil

water

metric ruler

2 Fill 4 foam cups with potting soil. Add water to the cups to moisten the soil.

3 Plant 4 of each type of seed, in its own cup, 1 centimeter deep.

4 Label each cup with the name of the seeds and the date you planted them. Put them in a sunny window.

5 Check the soil each day to make sure that it is moist, but not too wet. Add water when the soil feels dry.

6 Observe the cups every day until the seeds start to grow. Which was the first to show above the soil? Next? Last? How did this match with your ideas before you planted the seeds?

How Long Do Different Seeds Take to Sprout?

An Explanation

One thing that affects the time for a seed to start growing is the chemicals inside the seed. Different seeds have different chemicals to tell them when to start growing. Grass seeds usually grow very quickly, some just a few days after planting. It may take another kind of seed much longer.

FACT: In good growing conditions, Bermuda grass grows quickly. It can increase one tenth of its height every day. That is why it is often used in gardens and sports fields. It can also be a weed when it invades fields of food crops.

Bermuda grass

Another thing that affects the time is the amount of food (endosperm) in the seed. The more food stored inside a seed to feed the embryo, the longer that seed can take to start growing. A grass seed has less food stored inside it than either a radish or a cucumber seed. It has to sprout quickly so that it can begin getting its food from the soil and the sun.

Ideas for Your Science Fair

- What happens if you try to sprout seeds in the dark?

- Do radish seeds need water to sprout?

- How quickly do different grass seeds sprout?

Grass

Soybean   Carrot

Experiment 5
In Which Direction Do Roots and Shoots Grow?

When you plant seeds, does it matter what part of the seed points up or down in the soil? Write down your ideas and your reasons for them.

Now Let's Find Out!

Things You Will Need

cup of water

4 lima bean seeds

4 corn seeds

paper towel

zip-closing plastic bag

4 foam cups

potting soil

marker, pencil, and paper

metric ruler

water

1 Soak your seeds overnight in a cup of water.

2 Put the seeds on a damp piece of paper towel. Place the towel in a zip-closing plastic bag.

3 Keep the bag in a dark place until the seeds begin to sprout roots. (Keep the towel damp, and leave the plastic bag a little open so that the seeds do not get moldy.)

4 Label each of the cups as shown above.

5 You will plant two seeds 1 centimeter deep in each cup. For example, in cup 1, plant 2 lima beans with the root down. Water each cup as needed to keep the soil damp, but not wet. Write or draw what you think will happen in each cup.

6 Put the cups in a sunny window. Observe them every day for two weeks. Water the cups to keep the soil moist. Write down what you observe.

7 What happened to the shoots in the cups at the end of the two weeks? In what ways were the corn seeds different from the lima bean seeds? Why do you think the plants grew the way they did?

In Which Direction Do Roots and Shoots Grow?

An Explanation

In plants, roots grow toward the center of Earth. Shoots grow away from Earth's center. Chemicals in a plant's roots and shoots cause this to happen.

The force of gravity attracts the roots to grow in a downward direction. Even if you plant the sprouting seeds

FACT: Astronauts have experimented with plants in space. They found that plants far away from Earth's gravity do strange things. Some roots grow "up" and some grow "down." Some roots and shoots even grow sideways!

Space garden

roots-side up, the roots will still grow downward and the shoots will grow up.

 ## Ideas for Your Science Fair

- Is it possible to make a plant's roots grow upward?

- Is it possible to make a plant's shoots grow downward?

- What will happen to a potted plant if you turn it on its side?

Roots

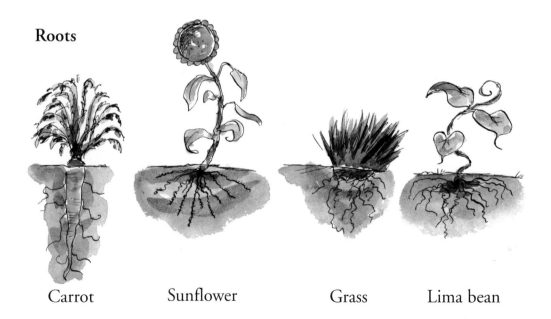

Carrot   Sunflower   Grass   Lima bean

Experiment 6
Which Seeds Have Oil in Them?

Warning: If you are allergic to tree nuts, do not do this experiment.

Some seeds people use for food contain healthy oils. Which seeds have the most oil? Write down your ideas and your reasons for them.

Now Let's Find Out!

1 Rub different types of seeds between your fingers. Which seeds do you think contain oil? Write your ideas down.

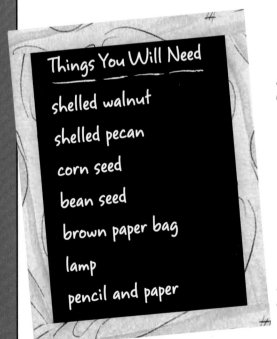

Things You Will Need

shelled walnut

shelled pecan

corn seed

bean seed

brown paper bag

lamp

pencil and paper

2 Rub half a shelled walnut on a brown paper bag. Hold the paper up to the light. What do you see? If there is oil in the walnut, you will be able to see light through the paper.

3 Test the rest of your seeds by rubbing them on different parts

26

of the paper bag and holding the bag up to the light. The seeds with oil will make a greasy spot on the paper through which light can shine. Which of your seeds seem to have oil?

4 Does one seed seem to have more oil than the others? How can you tell?

5 What other seeds can you think of that might have oil? Make a list and test them.

Which Seeds Have Oil in Them?
An Explanation

A seed contains food for the baby plant (embryo) inside it. Some of that food may be oil. When you rub seeds that have lots of oil in them on brown paper, the paper soaks up the oil. You are able to see light through the oily part of the paper. This is an easy way to test seeds and other types of food for oil. (Try doing this with a potato chip, for example.)

FACT: The chemist George Washington Carver (1864-1943) discovered dozens of uses for the chemicals in peanuts. These included cosmetics, dyes, paints, and plastics.

George Washington Carver

Humans and other animals can get energy from these oil-carrying seeds. We can squeeze these seeds to get oil out of them. Think of olive oil, peanut oil, grape seed oil, canola oil, corn oil, and many others.

 ## Ideas for Your Science Fair

- Is it easier to get oil out of seeds that are at room temperature or refrigerated seeds?

- Which seeds do squirrels seem to like more: those with lots of oil, or those without?

- Which seeds do sparrows seem to like more: those with lots of oil, or those without?

Experiment 7
How Well Do Seeds Grow in Different Soils?

What will happen if the same seeds are planted in different soil? Write down your ideas and your reasons for them.

Now Let's Find Out!

1 Fill each of 3 foam cups two-thirds full with different types of soil. Label each cup with the type of soil: Potting Soil, Yard Soil, Sand.

Things You Will Need

3 foam cups

potting soil, sand, and soil from a yard (you may need permission for this)

marker, pencil, and paper

water

packet of radish seeds

2 Add water to each cup so that the soil is just moist.

3 Plant equal amounts of radish seeds in each cup. (See packet directions to find out how deep to plant the seeds.) Put the cups in a warm, sunny window.

4 Observe the cups every day for at least one week until the seeds begin to sprout. Which seeds sprout first? Second? Last? Do they all sprout at the same time? Is this what you thought would happen?

How Well Do Seeds Grow in Different Soils?

An Explanation

Soil is a mixture of many things. The size of particles in soil can vary. Some are small, and others are large. Soil also has nutrients that help seeds and plants grow. Extra nutrients can be added to soil if needed. Radishes grow best in potting soil because it has small particles and added nutrients. Sand

FACT: Only about one fifth of the land on Earth is suited for growing food plants. In some places, water is added to help plants grow. Elsewhere, trees are cleared to make way for fields.

Food crops

has small particles, but no nutrients. Soil from a yard may or may not be good for radishes. It depends on the size of the particles in the soil and whether it has enough nutrients.

 ## Ideas for Your Science Fair

- Do bean seeds grow differently in different soils?

- Does adding fertilizer (like Miracle-Gro™) to soil make seeds sprout more quickly?

- Does finer-grained topsoil make seeds sprout more quickly?

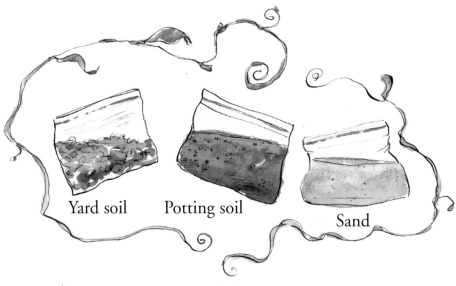

Yard soil   Potting soil   Sand

Experiment 8
Can Seeds Sprout in Cold Conditions?

Will seeds start to grow in different temperatures at the same time? Write down your ideas and your reasons for them.

Now Let's Find Out!

1 Soak 9 lima beans overnight in warm water.

Things You Will Need

9 lima bean seeds

cup of warm water

3 paper towels

3 zip-closing plastic sandwich bags

3 paper lunch bags

refrigerator with a freezer

alcohol thermometer

pencil and paper

2 Dampen 3 paper towels with water. Put a dampened towel inside each of 3 plastic sandwich bags.

3 Carefully put 3 soaked lima beans on the paper towel in each bag. Do not zip the bags all the way shut.

4 Put each plastic bag inside a paper bag to block the light.

5 The only difference between the 3 bags will now be temperature. Put one bag in the freezer, one in the refrigerator, and one in a warm place such as on a windowsill. Use a thermometer to read the temperature in each place. Write the temperatures in your notebook.

6 Observe the beans every day until they sprout. Which ones sprouted first? Second? Last? Did any not sprout at all? If so, why do you think this happened?

Can Seeds Sprout in Cold Conditions?

An Explanation

When the weather gets colder, plants do not grow as quickly, and they may lose their leaves. Cold weather also affects a plant's seeds. They need warmth to sprout. As long as it is cold, they will not sprout. The seeds you had at room temperature should have sprouted first. The seeds in the refrigerator should have sprouted later. Those in the freezer will not sprout.

Lotus seeds in their pod

FACT: Some maple seeds have to sprout within a couple of weeks, or they will die. But scientists have found that a seed from a lotus plant could still sprout after 2,000 years!

Seeds from many plants are not active in winter. They are "asleep," or dormant. When the weather gets warmer, the seeds are able to absorb water. Then they can sprout.

Ideas for Your Science Fair

- Where will lima beans sprout sooner: under a heat lamp or at room temperature?

- Do radish seeds sprout later in the refrigerator or at room temperature?

- If unsoaked seeds are put in the freezer for a week, will they still sprout when they warm up?

Experiment 9
Can Some Plants Grow Without Seeds?

Can you grow new plants without seeds? Write down your ideas and your reasons for them.

Now Let's Find Out!

1 **Put on rubber gloves.** (Swedish ivy sap can stain your hands.) Cut two 15-cm (6-in) pieces from the tops of both the Swedish ivy plant and the geranium plant.

2 Fill 6 clear plastic cups three-quarters full of tap water. Put a stem of the Swedish ivy cutting into each of 2 cups. Put the geranium cuttings into each of 2 more cups.

38

3 **Ask an adult** to cut out 2 potato eyes with one inch of potato flesh. Stick toothpicks into the sides of the 2 potato eyes. Balance the toothpicks on the last 2 cups so that the cut part of the potato is in the water, but the rest is sticking out of the water.

4 Observe the cuttings and potato eyes over the next 2 weeks. How do the plant parts change? Do you see plant parts growing that will make a whole new plant? Was this what you thought would happen?

5 If your ivy, geranium, or potato grows new roots and shoots, plant them in soil and see if they continue to grow.

Can Some Plants Grow Without Seeds?

An Explanation

Some plants can grow roots and shoots without seeds. Cuttings from these plants can grow roots if you put them in water. The tip of the plant is where most of the growing happens. Swedish ivy, geraniums, African violets, coleus plants, and many others can be grown from cuttings. Potato eyes will sprout new plants over time, too.

FACT: Nearly all fruit trees in commercial orchards are grown from cuttings rather than seeds. Growers take cuttings from plants that have good fruit so they can produce identical fruit.

Bartlett pears

The plants these cuttings produce are exact copies of the parent plant. In farming, this can be very useful for producing crops that look and taste the same.

 ## Ideas for Your Science Fair

- Will sweet potatoes sprout like white potatoes?
- Will leaves from maple trees grow roots in water?
- Can adding plant fertilizer to the water make Swedish ivy cuttings produce roots more quickly?

Swedish ivy   Honeysuckle   African violet

Experiment 10

Where Can You Find Seeds in Fruits?

Are all seeds located in the same place in a fruit? Write down your ideas and your reasons for them.

Now Let's Find Out!

1 Collect a variety of whole fruits. Do you think they all have their seeds in the same place? **Ask an adult** to cut the fruits in half. Make a drawing of where the seeds are. Are they all in the same place?

2 If you can, take the seeds out of the fruits. How are they the same? How are they different?

3 What other fruits do you know that have seeds like the apple? Like the peach? Like the lemon?

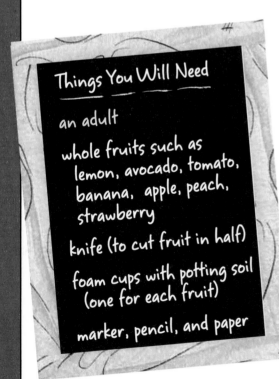

Things You Will Need

an adult

whole fruits such as lemon, avocado, tomato, banana, apple, peach, strawberry

knife (to cut fruit in half)

foam cups with potting soil (one for each fruit)

marker, pencil, and paper

42

4 How would you group the fruits that have seeds arranged in a similar way?

5 Try planting the seeds from the different fruits in cups of potting soil. Add water to the soil so that it is moist. Put the cups in a sunny window. Observe the cups over time to see if any of your fruit seeds sprout. Record your results.

Where Can You Find Seeds in Fruits?

An Explanation

Plant scientists group fruits according to how their seeds are arranged. The tomato, lemon, banana, and blueberry are all berries, because they have lots of small seeds inside. Many people call strawberries and raspberries berries, even though their seeds are on the outside! Scientists, however, call them aggregate fruits. Apples and pears, which have seeds inside in a star-like pattern, are called pomes.

FACT: Avocados were eaten in South America three thousand years ago. Scientists found avocado seeds buried with mummies. People may have thought that the seeds would provide food for the dead people.

Avocado

Fruit with a tough skin and lots of seeds inside, like lemons, oranges, and limes, are called hesperidia or citrus fruits. Fruits with one hard seed inside (peach, plum, apricot) are called drupes.

 ## Ideas for Your Science Fair

- Will seeds sprout sooner if you plant the whole fruit or if you take the seeds out and plant them?

- How do different fruits help to scatter their seeds?

- What is the best way to store and keep different types of fruit from spoiling?

 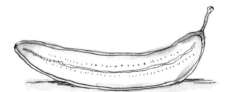

Strawberry (aggregate)   Banana (berry)

Apple (pome)   Peach (drupe)   Lemon (hesperidium)

Words to Know

burr—A spiky fruit that can cling to clothes or fur.

chemicals—Materials that make up all matter.

cotyledon—A seed leaf.

cutting—A plant part that can grow into a new plant.

dicot—A plant with two seed leaves.

dormant—To be in a resting state, usually in winter.

embryo—A baby plant inside a seed.

endosperm—The seed part that contains food for the embryo.

fertilizer—A mix of chemicals that help plants to grow.

gravity—The force that attracts all objects, such as roots, toward the center of Earth.

monocot—A plant with one seed leaf.

nutrients—The chemicals that plants need to grow.

roots—The parts of plants that take in water and nutrients.

seed—A baby plant, with its food and seed leaf inside its protective coat.

soil—A mixture of sand, clay, rocks, and other materials.

sprout—To send up the first shoot of a new plant.

Learn More

Books

Henderson, Joyce, and Heather Tomasello. *Strategies for Winning Science Fair Projects.* Chichester, England: Wiley, 2001.

Hewitt, Sally. *Amazing Plants.* New York: Crabtree Publishing Co., 2008.

Matthews, Rachael. *Seeds.* London: Thameside Press, 2005.

Robbins, Ken. *Seeds.* New York: Atheneum Books for Young Readers, 2005.

Internet Addresses

Glossopedia. *Plants.*
http://www.globio.org/glossopedia/article.aspx?art_id=30&art_nm=Plants

The Great Plant Escape.
http://www.urbanext.uiuc.edu/gpe/gpe.html

Encharted Learning—*Plants.*
http://www.enchantedlearning.com/subjects/plants

Index